POEMS

THE CONSEQUENCE OF MOONLIGHT

SOFIA STARNES

PARACLETE PRESS
BREWSTER, MASSACHUSETTS

2018 First Printing

The Consequence of Moonlight: Poems

Copyright © 2018 by Sofia M. Starnes

ISBN 978-1-61261-860-9

The Paraclete Press name and logo (dove on cross) are trademarks of Paraclete Press, Inc.

Library of Congress Cataloging-in-Publication Data

Names: Starnes, Sofia M., author.
Title: The consequence of moonlight : poems / Sofia Starnes.
Description: Brewster, MA : Paraclete Press, Inc., 2018.
Identifiers: LCCN 2017057155 | ISBN 9781612618609 (trade paper)
Classification: LCC PS3619.T3753 A6 2018 | DDC 811/.6—dc23
LC record available at https://lccn.loc.gov/2017057155

10 9 8 7 6 5 4 3 2 1

All rights reserved. No portion of this book may be reproduced, stored in an electronic retrieval system, or transmitted in any form or by any means—electronic, mechanical, photocopy, recording, or any other—except for brief quotations in printed reviews, without the prior permission of the publisher.

Published by Paraclete Press
Brewster, Massachusetts
www.paracletepress.com

Printed in the United States of America

praise for The Consequence of Moonlight

With uncommon prosodic and linguistic elegance, Sofia Starnes brings to the onetime familiar an exhilarating vividness, a [re]vision that avails the story's ongoing opening, continuing agency.

—SCOTT CAIRNS, author of *Slow Pilgrim:*
The Collected Poems and other works

Complexly ordered and layered, musically delivered, frequently profound, and brilliantly sensuous, Starnes' newest collection carries us through the life of humans and the life of Christ. Her deeply intelligent poems demand our attention and reward it with the wizardry with which she builds and shapes her lines. There is wit, too, and poems that respond to biblical and exegetical quotations. This is not an easy book, yet "[h]ow bruising-brave the larkspur's blue / becomes, how lover-heart // the roses—" Resurrection is here remade fresh, new, vital, and within grasp.

—KELLY CHERRY, author of *The Life and Death*
of Poetry: Poems and other works

How aptly titled *The Consequence of Moonlight* is. Here you will find a treasury of poems filled with an exquisite beauty and a kind of celestial music one rarely hears in contemporary poetry. But these lyrics, these songs, come with a warning with its invitation. Reader, you will have to slow down and allow the transforming moonlight of these lines to enter into your own sacred space. Starnes is at pains to erase herself as much as she can to allow the reader to discover something deep and profound within oneself. Welcome to a charged and grace-lit inner world, where you are not to put a name on everything you think you find here, but by warming yourself in this garden of delights might return a changed person, and the better for it.

—PAUL MARIANI, author of *Deaths &*
Transfigurations and other works

Although the answers to the big questions may be different for each of us, the questions remain the same, and Sofia Starnes is a poet who asks all the right questions. In the fine poems collected in *The Consequence of Moonlight*, we get a rare reward, the observations and insights of a talented and thoughtful poet attempting to examine the world through a spiritual lens.

—DAVID BOTTOMS, author of *We Almost Disappear* and other works

In her new collection, *The Consequence of Moonlight*, Sofia Starnes considers the nature of home, of children, of the creation where we live as creatures of God. In one striking line she writes, "God digs into his resurrection." And in these poems Starnes digs into the incarnation. Though the poems often seem ethereal and even otherworldly, basking in the reflected light of the moon, they have an edge. They mark that membrane shared by body and soul. I have written elsewhere that Starnes is part of the great tradition of poets, from Solomon to John Donne, who marry sensuality to religious belief. Her new poems remain part of that tradition. We are lucky to have them.

—MARK JARMAN, author of *The Heronry* and other works

For Bill, these poems, too, as always

I will put enmity between you and the woman,
and between your offspring and hers;
it shall crush your head
and you will strike its heel.

GENESIS 3:15

Now, a great sign appeared in heaven:
a woman robed with the sun,
and the moon under her feet....

REVELATION 12:1

CONTENTS

INVITATION   11

PART I

The Way We Thrive	15
The Other Room	16
The Gatekeeper	17
Tenebrae	18
By Name, We Called You	19
Elena Leaves Home	20
Emerge	22
Mortality	23
Mushrooms	25
Shadowcraft	27
Elena's Birthday Party	29
Survival at the Crossing	30
Beasts in Prayer	31
Close to the Tree	32
Elena by the Curb	34
Ancestry	35
Antechamber	37
Where the Clover	38
Whole	40

Elena, Halfway	41
The Search for Good	42
Unknowing	44
Elena Faces the Fire	46

PART 2

Last. Child. Last. Child.	51
After Departures	52
Archetypes	53
Lessons from Galicia	55
The Genes We'd Choose	56
Child's Mourning Lesson	57
Peddled Blooms	59
A Child's Gethsemane	60
Chaos Theory	62
Exodus	63
Catacomb	64
Survivor's Task	65
O Vivifying Bones	66
Dimas, Gestas	67
The bridal ferns,	69
The New World	70
God's Renter	72
The Corporal's Wedding	74
Anniversary	75
Lovers on Afton Mountain	77

Why Honeymoons Are Brief	78
Love Poem	79
A Mode of Permanence	80

PART 3

Meditation on a Lenten Corpus	83
The Consequence of Moonlight	87
Old Wives' Tales	89
Baptism of Desire	91
Tunnelers	92
And His Name Was Clemens	94
The Ways of Touch	96
Exhale	97
What We Know	98
White Crow	99
Child's Fruit	103
A Ghost's Progeny	104
Madurodam	106
A Viable Way Home	108
Elena Faces Halloween	110
The World You Make with Leaves	111
Another Life	113
After-Rain	114
Elena's Reprieve	115
Emmaus	117
Excess	118

Postponement	119
Love and the Afterlife	120
A Note to the Reader	122
Acknowledgments	125

INVITATION

Imagine one magnolia in the yard,
a solitary grosbeak out of reach
on a solitary branch—
the season's final archive of ascent.

Imagine that it drops a leaf.
Your glance catches it,
forgoes the arbor and the drift-wing
and the extent to which they live,

to reconcile the iris with one sky,
one tree, one mortal bird.
Intent, it's all about *intent*—
as with the eye, no more surveyor

but a lover in the momentary light,
or with the moon, drawn resolute
when tugging at the mist,
the immaculate lagoon, the girl

in mid-discovery.
At last, she stirs, full weight on little
feet, her focus on the door....
How green each word outside her room.

PART 1

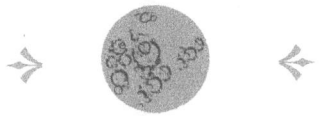

THE WAY WE THRIVE

The sun comes late in February or not at all,
but either way, our waiting rooms
are lit, and through a picture glass, an early

finch inches through molting.
Notice how close to restlessness she comes
(she knows little of resting);

think of unfinished nests, uncertain hands,
the impulse to outlast our hopes
in partial houses.   Of course,

this tells us only what we've learned
by living with the tenderness of need, as if
we were the small remedial weed

in a despondent garden.
It tells us only how a thing survives, how
we might thrive past sentinels. Sometimes

by clustering as nesting birds,
sometimes in duos, dusting up a path.
Even the dying leaf doubles its reach,
                    trilling to younger breeze.

THE OTHER ROOM

For this I pray—the room's proximity
whose distance is as venturous as kind,
calm in the evening, calling off

a silence I know best in increments. . . .
I do not seek it. For *after* is a word—
pressed, printed, turned leaf

to leaf in company.
For this I pray—our papered walls (linen
and grass) to bare new walls attached:

hall, piano parlor, welcome arch.
Oh, hear—the wind, the hustle-gold
of our forsythia spray—and eager feet,
                      not far.

    In my Father's house are many dwelling places;
    otherwise, I would have told you. . . .
         John 14:2

THE GATEKEEPER

Nowhere in reach of silence or dismay;
the word *arrest* will not endanger us
or leave us with a reliquary rose

too long inside its vase.
We will not see stray petals,
ambiguous avowals of a wish that's loose-

arrayed and seasonal.
Of course, there will be mayhem,
one afternoon when everyone's agog

because the earth is shaking,
because a single fault—
too far for dispensation and denial—

has ripped the old foundations,
and instead, the rooms and rafters smell
like burning moss

and mosses smell like peat.
       No. He will not let a fault—throat
of his own geography—speak out for him. . . .

For this is what we need not fear at all:
that he will lead us blindly
through a gate, sidestepping stones

and strangers, stems as streets,
and take us where we do not know a soul.

TENEBRAE

—the gradual extinguishing of candles

Our story waits its turn, as stories do.
You heard of it, one moment anxious to explore,
the other setting up the lamp you bought
to escape the coming

shadows.
    Once, on a twilight hill—
and so you slipped out in your walking shoes
and settled there, settled the prudent measure of a wick

to keep your lantern burning,
    But fires will lose their fingertips to singe,
and in the dark you'll shiver on your feet
and learn the cold of embers.

    Tenebrae. Tenebrae. *Here—*
It's where the story leads, of course:
in search of huddled warmth, from room to room,
stitch stretched to wanting stitch, full robes

from partial robes, remaking.
It's what redeems—*draw near—*
each retinue of souls who wait,
    wait nightly under scattered, scuttling comets.

BY NAME, WE CALLED YOU

      O dear descendant: every night
we watch you wander where the gas lamps burn,
the ones that flicker, one on one on one,

and call you by your name—
      which means the lamplighter will bring
repeatedly the unraveling of dark;

he'll draw one orange leaf against the curse
and shadow near and far.
      O dear descendant, you were given wealth—

scrolled, signed, and watermarked,
to settle bills with paper: half the debt accrued
      in war, the other calmly paid.

      This satisfies our need
to raise a true inheritor: a child for all eternity
by way of star and nightfall.

      Why pretend that strength resides
in millions? One world to match against our age,
one world, orbiting

      with this thought: You have a fortune—
count the lanterns, child—
the kind of fortune your ancestors made.

Walk up the sidewalk, wake it with your name.

ELENA LEAVES HOME
(Or: The Quality of Departure)

It's time, at last, to think about a girl—
the girl who changed the fortune of a road
by purchasing its shadows.

      Each morning she would drape
tendrils and vines on fences she knew well,
until the solid porch, the slatted steps,

gave way to thoughts of porches.
And so we said, reluctant from our gates:
Don't stay away,

no longer than it takes to wear out your perfume,
to count down stones and statuettes in rows,
to experiment with cobbles.

      After all, you are the same small child,
the same young girl,
the same contender for a pending pearl that bears

our own aurora. . . .
                By which we meant:
We know you best. We never have to imagine

who you are, never have to wonder why you wear
sandals on winter mornings.

    And when we see you flushed and hurrying

to mail a note, nothing but crinkly slush
under your feet, wishing up your painted toes,
the leather. . . .

There goes Elena—we say—we know her footsteps well.
There goes our child, she'll catch her death of cold.
          There goes our tenderest up the street.

EMERGE

At times this brings a stork, past rains, abandoning
a tower; at times a bubble dying
in a pond. I hear the word *emerge* and see a fern

or a feather; the first one wild and wispy,
to cure a wound, the role of ancient grasses; the other,
trail of a bird, slim fan or lady's purse—

the kind fairy tales gather.
Does not your heart, weary from things apparent,
ask what each storyline will tell,

which words carry their roots with candor?
Secrets would hunker down, safe in their winter castles,
were it not—

for the prophetic stem, weighty with beans
that rides its pole for air, for what we sense of seeds,
soft inches down, fussing our veins awake,

for every bone that pulls the body alert, to learn
its fragile face.
But what about our hands, the ones we excuse from light,

deep in our pockets?
With chambers dark, I think, the dark is change, is key.

MORTALITY

How can we live inside this house,
a house that knows the door is done,
that bones give what a bone
allows: a ribcage for a robin.

Too soon for spring (it says, it says),
but feathers lick the window sills,
and dogs yap, while their haunches dip,
swishing their eager tails.

How can we dream beyond the sun;
comfort in golden disregard, courage
in its resplendent gun, our screens
half-hiding orchids,

when, just before the sun's undress,
we pull a leaf to pull a birth—
our waking to the day's
address, where flagstones yield to moss.

From shadows and from lesser yields,
nightfall that confiscates
a room, I learn of bright, outlying
fields. . . . It will be fine; it will be fine,

to leave this rented consequence
with nothing but our borrowed feet,
to trade this skin—our reach, our dearth—
both sanctuary and residence,

far nearer to our bones than we,
                for vacancies in glory.

MUSHROOMS

This field is not a place
of loss; the mushrooms bow
uncartilaged, unheeding of the sun.
They swivel low under their lowly
tops and cup the earth for drink.

What is it like? To set the sterling
silver to a task without sufficient
tines, to guess at taste, forgetful
of a teaspoon's find or of a metal
boat against the tongue.

How would it be? To watch
the saints tell stories and not hear
about a woody morsel on their lips
(the turf in summer, vivid, between
sips): a common wince, a joy.

We wake to murk or moonlight
every night, squinting sometimes
at fog, sometimes at fingers faking
marquetry and trees. Where
nothing feels, nothing is ever real.

Heaven, I think, lives off our daily
skin, props us as sentient mushrooms
on our stems, stems over healing
wounds, wounds over soil,
over the gutsy bed of streams—oh,

    how the glorious body happens.

SHADOWCRAFT

Our room, complete with sorcerer and witch:
blessed was I as child—
the shadow-hand, a prowler on the wall;
the whisper of a drape, a serpent's hiss;

the mousetrap but a snap, a slipping.
The blush—blood on our cheeks
from fear or expectation—stayed adequate,
unspilled. It held its own, held willing.

We played with wizards too;
they were no wilder than a garden toad,
its leap against our bellies, tender pink, toe
webbings splayed and flat

before a childhood.
As nightmares went, ours would not hold
a candle to the tremors in far rooms,
hunters with ash-white hair and bone debris. . . .

Blessed were we as children, hugging fear.
For us, our nights did what a night must do:
point to a tree, now naked, on a field,
point to where, one day, we'll commend

our toys, and further off, rows of unopened
boxes. . . .   Ah, hold, hold, hold—
from prey to prayer, hold—
your little fear, your evening primed for hope.

ELENA'S BIRTHDAY PARTY
(Or: The Quality of Forgiveness)

Good night, Elena, of the pinpoint stars,
good night, young hostess in your corner
chair; the garden's empty and no guests
arrived: peekaboo, peekaboo. . . .

Two girls came, riding in their father's car;
they paused, a parody at your gate. Fair
game, they grimaced at the paper lamps:
half in glow, half in dark—a ring of curfew

lights. You lost them then, immersed
in bidding wars, to redder roses clambering
in other yards. No one slept over,
when the Dipper dropped: *Later, Elena, later.* . . .

        The early dew
is yielding futures now. A foreign car
rolls warily up your drive, and the myrtles
bow over two cautious heads. . . .

They don't remember you, or then, or why
                        you hold them tight.

SURVIVAL AT THE CROSSING

      Now barely are his bones alive,
now barely is the dragonfly a fire-
brand on his handlebars: gold tumbler—

The trucker missed him on his bicycle,
the boy's hand waving, banner-like,
dust, grease, and gallop over glossy tar—

a split-seed arrow. . . .
      Now ashen are his arms alive;
did you not see him on his bicycle,

before he pedaled through the crosshair
paths and sped, impervious?
      One body to each bend, O child.

(The trucker leapt out of his cab and cried,
cried blindly from a blind left eye.)

      Now brilliant are his bones alive,
and flitting is the dragonfly, over
the skid-and-start, the barely-a-scratch—

that hounds and hounds the trucker's heart.

BEASTS IN PRAYER

A caracole, a hoof, a hovering on grass;
the horse turns—painlessly, then pained—
and watches, warily, the wand.
Two sparrows drop; their wingtips pass

over this bloodless dance and miss it barely.
They come in peace, the rider knows;
his palms turn up, his motions mimicking a pose
of childhood: once pink, once holy.

A hound bays at the moon; its many feasts,
echoes of the things we long for:
the old sweet home, a heart for an address: sore
that at night awaits us. Oh, bless the beasts

whose moorings hold no doubt, no mask—
whose moon (like God?) spills on their grass,
unasked.

>   *Can you not buy two sparrows for a penny?*
>   *And yet not one falls to the ground*
>   *without your Father knowing.*
>   Matthew 10:29

CLOSE TO THE TREE

She knelt and prayed for birth,
and so the sparrows brought
(as birds often will do)
ribs from a perfect nest.
But then she specified, anxious

to make this true: *I need a body
of bones, a small and pinkish heart,
an ear for voices....*
        She prayed and asked
for words, something to mull and

chew, so ripe and succulent
her throat would grow a need
to be the human stem
that storms its way to seed.
        And so the phrases came,

out of a knotty root; she was no
longer shade, she was—part
need, part girl—
mumbling of an eternity
slim as a daylight page, slim as an

eyelash wick, too slender to be flare.
    And then she spoke of lips,
of kisses made for veins,
bodies that claimed a pulse
to keep their wrists from rest—

    restless, at last, this place
    for girls with godly aches. . . .

*   I fell on the same ground that bears us all,*
*   and crying was the first sound I made. . . .*
        The Book of Wisdom 7:3

ELENA BY THE CURB
(Or: The Quality of Detachment)

No longer there, where *country* is a tongue,
where hay lies heavy, where lofts grow hooks

from which to hang earth's instruments.
She's on her own: stranger to words like *scythe*

or *roost* or *rural*. And *threshold*, to her eyes,
is but pure pediment and gray, a pavement shelf,

the orphan edge of houses.
And yet the word rings true, as if, somewhere,

it still meant what it used to mean: a trampling
floor, gladness in grain and stubble,

a life that ends in bundles. It is as if such knowing
mattered.

But look; she has not lost it all. The girl wears
(God be praised) white open shoes, roped

soles, cream cotton laces, while under-
neath, the sidewalk combs loose particles of trees.

Thresh. Thresh. Hold. Hold.
        The leaves accrue a forest round her feet.

ANCESTRY

starts with a little leaf
that tells us how our bones
are like luxurious stalks
grafting in secret.
      Spring was the first behest;

berries to lure us home;
crabgrass to cross ourselves,
firefly or dragonfly,
and in the pregnant yard,
      patient eyes glimmered.

      Out in the yard, one voice,
one monumental cry,
loud in the setting sun, called
to a child up high, onto
a blue-green branch, with tangled

breezes.
      It spoke of golden gods,
ghosts meant to flabbergast,
kings, soaring saints, trances—
heroes with grit and throat,

thunder. . . .

But what we'll never hear
is what unnerves us most:
small footsteps scurrying home
after his trembling leap,

far, far from mouths of leaves.

ANTECHAMBER

Come night, we talk of heaven as a feast
for souls, supper at twilight and a crimson cloth

laid out between us; we speak of tender
lamb and honeyed sauce.

You'd think we'd walked into a rare event,
where friends help clear the tables when you've

had your fill, whispering: *there is always more.* . . .
A boy drops by with blackberries and plums;

he brings a word, some gossip, of a brand-new
flavor spilling out of a hand.

With eager lips and fingers he hails a covenant.
       I wonder why our talk of heaven often

dwindles there, before the dinner bell, the exotic
scents, the light over our shoulder—strong,

unspent—the delicate desserts.
Instead, we turn to finished meals and heirloom

plates, days set aside for dipping
and a tongue that aches for savor. Hungry. Real.

WHERE THE CLOVER

A sparrow does what sparrows
do: a chirp, a hop, a swoop:
no more.
        To say the lamb
fulfills its fold

by being, more than ewe, a hope,
gives wisdom
        that the wool has not:
the lamb goes
where the clover.

        And then there's this:
the dawdling dove,
white wingtips and her red-ring
eyes,
        a harbinger of peace.

She bears peace
like a contraband—slick carrier,
tongue against her beak—
        no wiser
than the dawn or dusk.

        Come,
see the sky the moon the sun,
        the non-erroneous olive
        branch
that falls on human hearts;

falls on the errand bird and
        bloom: they do not know
        the good they do,
or wonder how
            the good gets done.

WHOLE
(Or: The Quality of Assent)

Elena sets a napkin and a fork,
her plate, a tulip in between, and lastly,
on the cloth, a plastic spoon.

They wink and let her do.
How well she plays the solemn maître d';
how like a stork—part ancient, part

anew—their baby.
Mull less, mind more; she sets the table best
with bursts of energy, bounce of arrest

on her unfinished feet.
She's heard the spin: *God whistles*
with a countermelody, a message from his lithe

and lasting throat for brittle bones, for saintlings—
And thus, the words she knows
are wince and win. One cell pirouettes;

a second cell runs through the startling
hymn. A blush, a spark, a fusion: tip-top life.
Elena sets white napkins in the dark.

ELENA, HALFWAY
(Or: The Quality of There)

Not every shadow wears ash on its sleeve,
        not all our Wednesdays cinder-

knit their brows, some labor under orange dust
        to leap across cloud cover.

Elena thinks the night's a harvest bowl,
        the moon, a fruit susceptible to bleed:

she stares up hard, hard at its bumpy skin.
        The sky is thirsty.

Elena's learned a new word: *equinox*,
        a blade to wield between opposing fields

(and yet there is no war, no war at all).
        The red she sees ends as all skirmish

ends, extending nightfall on her human
        fear. Come, swallow whole your share

of grief, for no one pushes off with half
        a heart, or half an awe,
                or half the obliging lung.

THE SEARCH FOR GOOD

She said she'd search for Good
outside the house that raised her
predictably, assumed—

as bloomed in rose and wealth,
a wealth of ease at morning
when everything that spilled

spilled out from knotless spools.
Her mother called—she loved her;
Her father left each dawn,

yet slowed down at the corner
and caught up with her fear.
All's well, he'd wave back, nodding;

All's well.   He would return
before the kitchen heated, before
the rooms collected

long hours of worrying.
She left to search for Good
beyond the words "apparent,"

"full-grown," "wholeness," "prolific"—
the bated breath of innocence
in iridescent rooms.

Outside, against her shadow,
a rose opens—exhumed—
            expecting to be red.

UNKNOWING

A red car rolling down the street,
        a woman for whose memory it calls,
the carriage of a husband's freckled hand—
        this, only, at her reach.

Beneath the red car, solid are the wheels,
        their tread, inheritor of yield;
beneath release, some gravel and some tar—
        a winding road, the ribbon of conceal.

What we have lost is no more than what we
        abandon (like a vestibule) at birth;
there's moisture in each palm suggesting rain,
        and August every spring.

We might forget the hammock in the yard,
        or how to lie reliant,
how low the branches, how profuse the air
        with bright red apples dangling.

But if they fall, we shall remember *thud*,
        and with each peel, the aftermath of *leave*.
Touch me, my love. For knowing reconvenes
        as constancy.

We had a birth, a life of fingertips.

    How do we know?

        How, but through trembling.

ELENA FACES THE FIRE
(Or: The Quality of Oblation)

I

>His. It is her wish to be His. Though once, when she was feverish, He could have laid a palm and calmed the fire, but didn't. When she walked out the door, into another room, the one where circuits sparked, He could have shown His face, the one with honeyed beard, but didn't. When every wall collapsed, flame coating steel and glass, He could have rained on them, but didn't. When every curtain dropped, wearing cinder and ash, He could have swept the dust, but didn't. How could she wish to be His?

II

>Yet in a place called Heart,
>the choice is this:
>embalmed or resurrected,
>she'll wander to the side
>
>of Him who, in a corner,
>pockets a chestnut's flesh
>hot from a fire,
>from angry sparks and embers.

He thumbs the soot,
once, twice,
and for a caring hour,
its creamy cheeks, uncharred.

III

Fires are different here. They start as good.
    Hearth, chimney, logs; crackle, cinder, wood.
Fire on these stones is like a fairy at home.
    Heat. Light. This continent where kindling roams.

IV

She lost her ring in embers, after the fire.
Small. Tough. An emblem. To no one, worth—
not to the cat who moused it, nor to the dove
whose beak broke cleanly, against

that hardy ring, now silent in soil and fire,
years after celebrating her going forth.
Flames turn her day to fireside, to love-
hung room, where life means waiting, caressed.

For our God is a consuming fire.
Hebrews 12:29

PART 2

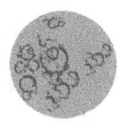

LAST. CHILD. LAST. CHILD.

We do not speak in tongues or hold séances—
hands on a table,
ear to a distant hymn, as if our ghosts were nimble
advocates of speech. Away from trances,

we believe in the close-knit village
of our voices; rarely believe in voices
we can't hear.   A word depends on impulses—
air-catch, air-lease—that hold its meaning hostage.

Language, like the dawn, is the defeat of hours
and a second's gain, to look at new geraniums
and say, timelessly: *pink thumbs*:
two words that leave the womb as flowers;

it is to hear, inadequately, words like "last"
and "child," in threat of twilight. *Say it again,
please*: "Last. Child. Last. Child." While a judgment
rides home to its homecoming. Shouldn't we ask

who and why, the plot and the denouement, the ache
for endings? One child's asleep now;
             the other's fitfully awake.

AFTER DEPARTURES

To see the soothing mud tracks—
they were here—
and hear a foreign language turned to clay,
for clay is good for familiarity;

the circus closed last night for the last time
and cockatoos rejoiced—
how strange to us,
compulsive lovers of proximity;

we thought them pleased,
night after tinsel night,
green echoes of our pleasure and our search,
as wingless children, ruffling differently.

ARCHETYPES

They never were, they always are—
these children who run heaven in our midst,
who populate our parks,
who lose their daily grit on graveyard walks
but find it in the gravel of their shoes.
We are far stronger than you are, they think;
We are alive and you are not.

    I never met them, but I always knew
    the tawny moths that fevered on their cheeks.

You've heard me say "Elena" for a girl,
and "Carlos" for a faraway young boy;
they run home, so the rule says,
when it rains,
they rush off, so my eyes fear, when it storms.
They play, unpausing, with the village brood,
where children seem less clear, less separate—

    I never met them, but I always knew
    about the notes their oyster-pockets hold.

What do they say?
How do they pick the words?
I'm sure that Carlos clamors his in haste—
he, of the archetypal kind,
who'll lift a sword without excessive qualm,
but who remains a child before the dark.

When shall I draw them out, free from the woods,
he and Elena, and others, fresh from myth?
When will their muddy feet, heard two by two,
turn to the open air of Burnley?
That day, they'll cease their darting in and out,
and come in pairs (or halves) as humans do—

>They live in houses, light their fires, and dream
>about the world, how it will come to be.

LESSONS FROM GALICIA

The quiet house of nature grew
before you learned to speak,
before you thought of boys and girls,
before a sempiternal ache,

while stirring up an ancient town,
ventured into an open spire
of flesh and bone, of discreet cells
and spacious, indiscreet desire.

Nature—in nodding—gives her name
to every ladder rung she draws,
rigor and rustle at each step:
there may you rise; there may you pause;

there will you gaze out to a life
you imagined in Galicia, when friends
with wiser dreams would say:
> *go, find some kindly kindred saints*

> *whose hands are filled with stories.*

Ah, stories you'll need
to greet a boy, to live a life, to love a child,
to spell the moon, to heed

> the sempiternal word
> your ache already knows above.

THE GENES WE'D CHOOSE

The lifting mist; a curtain lifts: remnants of a sail.
Happy the stowaways that sail.

I am addicted to those fans over the doorways,
clear symbols out of glass. What name does each

entail?   Once there were diamonds on a ship,
the fleers of catastrophes—young boys in caps

and girls with veils. . . .
Watch them, leaning on the bowsprit toward East.

Some centuries turn children into birds and perch
them on a boat's rail.

The 19th was like this, when generations hithered,
descending in a circular array: cousins,

second-kin—a heart's trail.
Blest are the hands and ankles wreathed in beads—

blest, too, the errant gene, the rib that runs away
from ribs, the bones in dark detail.

O wise turned wiser with a child's breath, once
more to sea when roots fail. Speck in the blue, feet

      on a deck, in time to raise the young sail.

CHILD'S MOURNING LESSON

Thin cedar roads, white tables, and a stone,
        the sandalfoot Madonna and a text: *bury*

the dead, carry your bread as givers,
        serve it warm. . . . This was the heart

of it: a destiny for us,
        to temper death with sweet cakes.

Some days she'd tell us more: you'll
        feed your steaming suppers to the weak,

extend a canvas tent over their cots, console them,
        night through night. . . .

Catch me if you can! we'd say—
        children with ruby elbows, in cahoots,

mortal as skin, digging our perfect teeth into a life,
        and thinking: young, impervious.

Now, late but true, a latch lifts off what is:
        the woman, here; the gardener and blooms,

green zest, where we ran. . . .
        I'm sure *he* was the one: the story's savior

on whose words we tumbled, twilight hoops;
    on whose words she urged us:

gather the crumbs, give them a kiss, be good.

Blessed are those who mourn:
they shall be comforted.
    Matthew 5:5

PEDDLED BLOOMS

From door to door, the air stirs young,
though nothing we might resurrect is new;
the boy who sells his bulbs and rhizomes

is pedaling through. A spill of wares,
a realignment of copper and skin;
a label on each tag to test his fingers.

> Shouldn't this childish peddling
> comfort the earth?

Look close at the vine on our window ledge;
we blow, and the leaves turn, tumble,
make consummate sense.

So near: their measured purchase of light,
the price that lengthens their stems:
slim matter; the coin, paid and set aside,

commerce of lungs. The world survives
through barter, it seems. *Is that the doorbell?*
A boy stands, breathing the blooms he sells.

> *I bless you, Father . . . for hiding these things*
> *from the learned and the clever*
> *and revealing them to little children.*
> Matthew 11:25

A CHILD'S GETHSEMANE

They thought their garden safe, in leafy-evening
dark, under their sneakered feet, guarded

by guardian stars. Magnolias flecked the walls
with oval locks, a gleam, sudden their leaves

and sleek, as spears and trouble. . . .
There was a hidden bench, smoothed out of handy

stone, where he—their father—sat, while they
played badminton; while they cried "twenty-one!"

and in the twilight won.
Then came the piercing eye of a colossal moon;

it burnt his restful head; it struck his neckline weave,
his shirt: the Adam fruit traveling down his throat.

They thought their garden safe, but they no longer
played where giant men ran through,

their kisses kept in check, for kisses might declare
a war that would happen.

Unless new saints arrived, unless they hurried forth;
the garden stoked alive; the children scooped

in droves, history at their heels, in heels of home. . . .

> *Listen: the time will come—*
> *indeed it has already come—*
> *when you are going to be scattered.*
> *John 16:32*

CHAOS THEORY

And who parades a placard down the streets,
and whose cartoon bruises the nacre air,

who paints the now abandoned steed with carrot
mane and spurs and nickel hoofs,

who acts the wizard, who the jinx, who sinks
to save a carousel and play under its reel—

Who meets each prisoner and sings, who hums
into their shirts, a low cry over almed, awaiting

fields?   *Ah, maddening as spoofs without a song,
maddening this need to make sense of.*

The blouse I wear blushes into the wash;
red is the kerchief dripping on the line. I'll pick

the berries Eden gave away, fruit juice
and perfume tincturing.   I'll say: we understand

this once—anthology and roots, all about signs
and circuses and rifts.   Holy is the scent

that gives the body away, the body, a cruet
tipping, tipping oil. Holy is our skin—I know it:
                                           life amongst.

EXODUS

The young they bear, now tightly tucked aboard.
A full moon finds their breath, no longer rush
but stillness. They know the stillness

for what it brings. *How many tadpoles*
will the waters hoard, how many—from their stasis—
rush ashore, push forth, and rise in shallow grasses?

The young they keep, slim shelter in the foam
that swirls about them, as if in rough white collars.
Above, rain pours and pours with native clamor.

Sometimes it is the rowdiness they flee,
the re-arrest of choruses at dusk, rising to brim and
back, crucifying spring. Sometimes it is

an alley's plight, its anger.
And everywhere, of course, the crowds keep reeling,
reeling at their feet,

a deadly dance for tadpoles. . . .
How many children can an eddy yield? The small hands
cling and cling, their fingers fixed on salvage.

CATACOMB

> *Ozra Momenadi, 80, was pulled out of the rubble,*
> *almost a week after the earthquake hit the region.*

How she rose—as a violet from Eden, from a world
in love with petals, firm and fresh, beyond

a doubt. *Is the night a ring or aphid?* Her ascent
shifted the gates, where the workmen hurled

down, downward, terrified. Not a sound
from a catacomb turned crib, just the filigreed event

of her wrinkles, her skin's gingery design.
She was 80, 85, and they pulled aloft her bloom, 6 days

after they'd secured babies, sucklings in dry
aprons. *God be praised.* No one, no one asks as much

from our children. *They're our gold;*
they're our treasures. So she rose, dreamy, and her eyes,

unbeknownst to dove or raptor, adolesced—
Oh, a century as egg; under veil, a ribcage hatches.

> *The place is too cramped for me,*
> *make room for me to live.*
> Isaiah 49:20

SURVIVOR'S TASK

Few in her neighborhood will understand
exactly what her fingertips afford; she
kneels beside the river, dips her gourd in water
(what she knows of undulating life).

She saw him leave, the cortege on the banks:
souls loosely laced, as loosely as the flock
of geese they followed. She heard their talk,
before the hush of leaving. And in their

wake, she lost her courtship with the world,
the reason for a touch. That's when
the river rose outside her door; it's when
the waters hummed: *Are not the currents*

in your hand the currency he hungers?
And so she stayed, conspicuous her gait,
a woman sorting artifacts: the cobalt ewer tipsy
on the ledge, the cup still wet

at noontide. With every heft, the narrative
of hills; with every fissure, nightfall.
And yet there's this: the birds she saw that night
have drawn a flat line in the sky, a fine horizon

calling. No wonder she grows eager to retell
her finished part: caress, absolve, unshell.

O VIVIFYING BONES

For all that's well and done, a mask
might mar their peace, though nothing should it be,

but hope of pure, fine faces—
For all they understood, their backyards beckon, new:

a hosta bed, the woods, then silvery eruptions
of incendiary seeds . . . from there to grow a flower,

a flame-dispensing vine, whose stems bespeak of spears
and the return of warriors.

For all the prayers they said, the field attrition
ceased; the trenches veered to truce,

and in the truce they worshipped as children made
of earth. For all that's done—unsaid—

at last, they're coming home to fresh-raised, fresh-tilled
hillocks, stepping with bootless toes,

stepping with fears of crushing
        —O vivifying bones;

one soul to every abode, over the crimson mountains.

> *How beautiful on the mountains*
> *are the feet of the messenger announcing peace. . . .*
>   *Isaiah 52:7*

DIMAS, GESTAS

If she'd known more about them:
who the wiser, who the one born late, on Saturday,
his father, from a summer field, gregarious.

If she'd known who would be the brighter and who
the cold and solemn winterer—
would she have borne them equally?

Would she have pooled their cells with waterfall
abandon?
      The earth wakes daily enamored,

dazzled by the red fuzz on her hills, the sun
separating cedars, valley roads, ducks on a white lake.
And though no servant cooks her breakfast for her,

though no one combs her hair,
she sets the day for brews and breads,
for women stewing figs to glaze their timely hungers.

      And so the babies come, one after the other.

Now, tell me again, which child awoke
out of which pregnant hour? Who tumbled first;
who followed, sweetness to mouth

to flower?   She knows both left her,
left her reservoir of labor, mingling strangely on a tree.
She knows—both hung through eventide—
need rescue.

> *The Lord never goes back on his mercy,*
> *never cancels any of his words.*
>   *Ecclesiasticus 47:24*

THE BRIDAL FERNS,

    the pigeons, and our lives: they multiply
near streams, near roots, off summer
suns and vanquished vapors from some long-lost

    star that never pulled itself, was pulled apart
by rival concubines and gravities,
blazing until its permanence must turn to pit.

    I wonder how such puny a word as *pit*,
could be both seed and slum, both dormant agency
and tomb; both conflict verb—met up against—

    and scoop; a stone that yields, yields small,
yet hurts the hand. I wonder how,
but pittances deceive: thus is the way of potency

    and plea; the soil is notched by hooves
and by the Fall, and then by falling fledglings,
insecure.

        How measured is the earth for gift and scar,
        for creaks and croons, for the precarious child.

THE NEW WORLD

A tiny resurrection brewed
feeding the lamplight at our door,
and in its shadow burned our need
to send out parties to the moon,
wide open in her swollen hours. . . .

There, in a small suburban shore,
a frozen track, a bleached white flag—
we laid the blueprints of a town,
thin louvered blinds and frontal
stones; there we arranged our green-

house domes (among thin mannequins
and stores), tulips in ornamental
glass, to gaze at from our windows.
But that was then (the leaves, now dark)
outlying has become outlast,

dust of our glossy enterprise
in an abandoned plaza. Once more,
the sails, the sweetheart ships; once
more, our skillets wrapped in silk,
our bluest sandals pressed to rest

in a distant carbon village.
The earth, white porch or blest
tempestuous town, must blow her final
farewell kiss. . . .
She will not fret too much, I think,

how far we go, how burnt our reach,
for near the edges of her streams,
her caves are set for evening fires:
there lie her children, wound in sleep,
their fathers watch and wait and keep.

GOD'S RENTER

Somewhere between a ghost
and ghost-relief, between the gas-lamp flickers
and a stoop—a house behind the ragged

thickets.
Somewhere beside a kitchen
and a hall, from chair to chair, where travelers

hang their cowls, still damp
after their countless vigils.
          She's come into a house that someone

owns; she's made it hers—as if through acronym—
and thinks of lost mail in a postal slot:
(her God's, her quiet host's,

whose threshold hurts, is mending).
He is quite happy, actually,
to leave mortality and creation to this bride,

to write her little notes about a dish, to send her
flowers when the rent is due,
redeemed.

And of the neighborhood?
They rarely hear of landladies and lords;
they are all root, all home. They set their shoes

precisely by their beds; they lean aboard
their evening balconies; they mail their checks.
O daily soul:

who better breathes the wholesale of your room?
Who best exhales your wishes?

> *The Spirit and the Bride say, "Come!"*
> *Let everyone who listens answer, "Come!"*
> *Revelation 22:17*

THE CORPORAL'S WEDDING

Tight, tightly willed, this bliss: the foyer's hanging
basket and its moss, a garland banister, a silver clockface

ticking into glass. Here, promise and delay occur,
as in a wedding where the bridegroom slips, fumbles

the ring, and turns the day to segments, finger-thin: a piece
to keep. He loves her, loves the birdcage presence

of her ribs, their momentary kisses.
Should they make haste—elusive bodies—steal away,

toss off her tulle, in a run? Would this distress her, discon-
certing? (Nobody knows, as he, the creases

crosses make, the skins they stain.)   Tight, tightly
still: the moss that meets a blood-kin entourage, the boy

on twilight leave. The foyer locks its dark anemones;
once scars—lanterns, O heart!—now sentinels on knees.

> *For God created human beings to be immortal,*
> *He made them as an image of his own nature.*
>   *The Book of Wisdom 2:23*

ANNIVERSARY

She has known him fully blessed—lover
in a fine translucent suit, on a low and fruitful

barge. It was Sunday after Mass, dance of candles—
and they satisfied the bells. Seventeen.

She will not forget the clouds from the backlot
of the church, crescent pink—arise, arise—

like the resurrected gauze of a savior . . . lance
of herons, flock of saints.

Was the wedding party caught in their flurry?
Were the guests gregarious, too?

Seventeen. All these years, a charity has scattered
roses, pillows, sugar on the chin.

All the years, their gravity has lifted, airy.
That day cleared into a sieve, but who cared?

Craze a joy, fall asleep in a clean absorbent cot,
trick the midday, wake upon. Seventeen.

Nights, she knows an almost-loss, with a mossy mat of peril on their heads, at the dew point.

And she leans back to the sieve, thinking: *residue!* Out of marmalades, a sheen—

> *The new as well as the old,*
> *I have stored them for you, my love.*
> The Song of Songs 7:14

LOVERS ON AFTON MOUNTAIN

The sun, omnipotent—for whom all children rise—
is now a slender broth that drips
over a cliff. The sky pours out this meal

on unfamiliar creatures. But no one dares to drink.
And now the road's a spoon tilting its face,
until the lovers pause, and sit,

and hug their knees.
A panoply of weeds is feuding at their feet, pinned
between road and rock—and overhead, a star.

They've come mostly to watch,
but now they fall asleep, where no one speaks
or shouts, while caravans of thieves

tiptoe into the houses pinioned to lower fields.
Theirs is no fool's alarm:
bold fingers round their ribs, their bonus breaths,

their pluck, the shore-away of shivers. . . .
They do not know they're meek—
hushed into powerless—from star to star, complete.

WHY HONEYMOONS ARE BRIEF

Although the evening light outflames their room,
although it skims their shadows on the rug
(a rug of Indian oceans and tall reeds),
and warms the woolen hollows—

And though they lie on skeins and stare up high,
as if the spackled ceiling were the dusk,
and underneath, a calendar of streets,
a temporal bemusement—

Although the finished spread seems nothing
but the burgeoning of tender, tender touch,
they learn what we once learned:
there's nowhere far.

A restless voice cries out across the street
and steals what twilight gives them, tipping earth;
the dual scents of lamb and mint converse,
and mindless of the door, feasts wander in.

No matter if they pull the shades, latch inwardly
the locks; the world must sneak its aches, its carbon in.
Won't one of them respond: cheeks risen, feverish?
And won't the other pray with human breath?

> *Wisdom concealed, and treasure undiscovered,*
> *What use is either of these?*
>   *Ecclesiasticus 20:30*

LOVE POEM

It may be cold—for some, too cold—
this hemisphere of thrifty seeds;
I have not seen a dragonfly
or caught the hungry hummingbird.

And still an hour has dwindled by
without a ripe accomplishment;
it may be cold, no doubt too cold
to catch the hungry hummingbird.

The summer was for dragonflies,
as poignant as our childhood things—
the come-and-go of gorgeous wings
in hemispheres of thrifty seeds.

It's not for us to worry now;
there is no late, there was no soon;
first shiver, and the cavalcades
of earth breathe undercover.

It's winter but our body's reach
is equal to its task. In you, my love,
those gorgeous wings, in you the rush
for handheld things, outlasting husks

and hemispheres, while *we* outlast them.

A MODE OF PERMANENCE

Caress me into long life; life *is* long,
if we're to rise from swallowtail and thorn,
green ivy and a muddy tolerance for death.
Caress the ribs where solitude

is born. Eternity slips in as something else:
new skin for our elusive shadows;
a cut-rose blooming on; a mirrored piano,
songs for a different hour. . . .

Don't you see? Our house will yield yet
shield our first embrace; the walls will laugh,
when voices fall, heavy; in time, we'll
decorate a place. Always.

And when we lift our rings out of a ritual
burial, we'll bite the glint, the gold—
still ours, this mode of permanence—
now naked, now heaven-kissed.

For you have said: love is built to last forever.
Psalm 89:2

PART 3

MEDITATION ON A LENTEN CORPUS

I – THE SCULPTURE

With neither lift nor spring, his shoulders clumsy,
large, he reaches up, from the root-ball of his feet

to a rising, solitary arm-ache. Out of the pines of some
Virginia farm, out of a pine-heart saved from a barge

that carts debris to Brooklyn; out of the work
of stubbed and stubborn hands—

      here to stay, the wood-nails driven through
his palms, the body hunched. It might have been—

why not?—that the Rabbi had thick and curly hair;
that he was stooped,

that as a child he bent far too often to receive:
scoop, touch and bandage this and the other's affairs—

malleable men, mild widows. Oh, it must take time
for a word to settle within each curve,
                              inside the wood's *idea*.

II – THE CARVER

The sculptor wept (I know) and wouldn't think *idea*
the right word, more like a wind, a 30-mile-an-hour squall

met lately. It pinioned pines and flung tree limbs,
homewards. *Feel.* The red photinia shivered, as did

the pyracantha thorning from seed. *Feel.* Fire, twig, nail
on twilight brick, a pending rescue.

The thumb knows reason. Didn't we learn from ridge and
dimple, Adam's apple, cog of a wheel? Heartache.

The man is losing his sight from pressure;
he sculpts with both hands, resin and oil—oblique light

on rosette and ruckus. Not flash, but *feel*, grasp, gauge, glory.
Throb and texture.

I'll keep him company; listen to the thud-thud of the darker
night he's working through, ever against never.

III – FRIDAY

And when a breeze no longer blows, when talent
in the air falls short—no buzz, none to tantalize a hope—

his muscle trips, misses, and he hungers for better wood:
Forgo and give;

your life is now near spent, this afternoon's your tool.
                        In Oregon, a silent continent away,

a woman leans over a well that used to fill each spring,
to seek her eyes, to know herself upon. The air is heavy,

and she forgets why, where. The well dries up;
the woman prays into the loss; her sleeves catch, earnest

on the rim, once wet, now stone on fire.
Love, love her, too; for where the sun sets, rumoring,

the day is good. Close to a tree, over a well,
                        a common God to summon.

.

IV – RESURRECTION

One day, this Corpus will not be; I won't know how
he looked: sunlight on liquid beard, wood-thread and

polish. Somewhere else, wavering, I'll tell whoever crooks
my elbow: *slowly, please* . . . while I tinker

with a stowaway remembrance stealing back: joy or
dread that swells the empty.

It is not memory that makes us, not the spellbinding lace
on nitty-gritty nerve-ends. (How mistaken I was!)

I fall asleep and am; I miss a name (not Peg, not Rose),
still I am; I lose a thought in a heart-shaped pillow, and. . . .

Your cheek is what my thumb repeats, what carries—
curlicue and stem—beyond remembering.

I'll press it; part need, part instinct—no, *all* instinct, true
as genuflect love. Lose and God gives.
                                    So ready, ready to resurrect.

THE CONSEQUENCE OF MOONLIGHT

The consequence of moonlight
is a sigh, and saints out in the garden, strong
and pure, lift stories, as if bodies,

to the sky. They show up every evening—
undisguised—when evening stars are fewer,
when every light's

a consequential sigh.
They look around: their faces multiply
and dare the ghosts our statuaries secure,

lifting each bodied story to the sky. . . .
What calls them to our yard? With them, we try
"aloft" and "lamp" for meaning,

though this lures us to inconsequential lights.
And so, from word we turn to wordless,
falling short of the full, heaving

breath. . . . (Would it ensure
a lifted body stories up the sky?)
Whether we speak or not, if nights should

pry us open then disperse and fail to endure,
these saints will lift our consequence,
our sigh—
their moonlight bodies storying up our sky.

OLD WIVES' TALES

Full moon: we never plant against her gravity,
nor hammer nails, whose necks crane
steely above a tide. Full

moon: new babies come in threes,
and gunshot wounds fill up the trauma center
with mixed cries.

Is that a baby purring in too pure a sky
or a disheveled drunk still mulling?
We pray them far apart, as if the wail

of hounds beyond a parking lot
might rise to hurt us. *Come to think of it.* . . .
Full moon:

an evening links sobriety to wolves—
and we escape madness.
The risk is from that hanging satellite, of course.

Who'd love and still be sane under unblinking
lanterns? Who'd say: watch how my bones
evolve, out of their fur to kindness?

We're not alone, less than a flight away
from lofty bodies. *Look!*
Someone has fixed the shutters, and the moon—

now ghost, now girl—now breathes, now utters.

> *No more will the sun give you daylight,*
> *nor moonlight shine on you,*
> *but the Lord will be your everlasting light. . . .*
>   *Isaiah 60:19*

BAPTISM OF DESIRE

By way of longing, winter has its eye
on red wings negotiating timber limbs,
blood-rose and tailwind from the winter
bird: and nowhere nest, and nowhere

rest for saints. This I would see and call it
my concern. But only if I'd cradled her;
her feathers tufting, eager to be spared—
and nowhere nest, and nowhere rest

for beasts. Apocalyptic is too long a sigh,
the evening light translates to evening
wind. Again, an eye on whirled and wintered
bird. Awareness is the proper name for nest.

Restless we live; a penknife scrapes a ply-
wood, hinges harp; thud is the shutter's
grim reminder that it shakes. The world's alert
to feelings and to flukes. Until, confessed,

we hunger for the birds.

TUNNELERS

I

The geese have come with glaciers
on their feet,
grey wings and winter eyes,
artful in early sun and cold debris.

Come April, life is easily their cry
trumpeting worlds up-close
and worlds that bolt out of my reach.
The tunnel nears. . . .

II

Town on a cliff; lives in a cave;
wheat in a mill; babies to save.

III

Between the bands of geese,
the men work on the road; their arms
are vein and mountain, brown
and slick: each rock, a rendered Adam's

rib, each bruise, the consequence
of wills. They think of runs and meets—
the tunnel deep;
their railing holds the ribbon of this race.

IV

Children on wheels; vines up the fence;
beaks rattling, where the metal bends.

V

Come April, we are nothing,
nothing like the birds—
we need one face, one urgency up close:
we dare not fly: the sky is rare with geese.

AND HIS NAME WAS CLEMENS

Not a hope left in his body
when he came home, undoing huckleberry
petals one by one, downriver—

why should it matter a hundred years later,
beyond the lost fluff of his disenchanted head.
A thought, that is all there is, he said,

and stretched his weary remnant on white
wicker. White shirt, white skin, white
suit: casings for an imagination

that went from cause to caustic.
But who am I to know. I grew up miles away,
saying grace before rice kernels, plastic

bowls, and penitential guava.
I read idly then, about the freckled boy on a raft
and the black man meandering downriver,

while all the while, our rain gathered in drums,
our moon in bowls, our sky in a pond
for wading.   Not enough rage in my life,

between blue curtains and Cápiz squares;
not enough rage underneath the bed
for the lost marble. Not enough loss or against,

not even when a flood crushed our sagging
porch with soil, then spilt again.
    Mercy, that is all there is—we'd say,

whenever someone stayed
long enough to hold our tumid heads, kiss off
the sweat, the silent sparkling brows,

        and mean *forever*.

THE WAYS OF TOUCH

    Here's how you know the urgency of touch:
one day you see a nest about to fall and fledgling birds

turn tiny wings upwind: a breeze at hand to bear them
to new houses.   In this,

a near assurance that we meet, that every cedar felled
against the green may grow into a town. In coastal

cells, in rows, a cluster of inhabitants, their kiss.
    A woman bears a basket on her head; from daily,

heavy laundering she comes, her palms up high,
the late sun tracking notions: a husband's shirt, a skirt,

a blanket for their baby. And though the rigors
of their village toils are past, the ways of touch persist.

    Glass often breaks to smithereens, a crystal screen
may crack against a thumb; sapphire to dust:

dispersals. . . . And still—between restrain and urgency—
you are the child a woman blanketed each night,

the one who would not hurry. And she, the mother
    for whose arms, all hours, you cried.

EXHALE

The summer breaks when August turns
fifteen, and she, of kindest flesh, wonders about
the wind that whips outside the house,
that calls the boys inside, that thins the sheen
of exhales on her lip. A blind
unrolls (for Palestine has blinds); her blouse

reworks her ribs; her parchment motherhood
is waterskin, and clings to particles
of sweat, to steam above the stove.
Is there a buzz? An emissary of sorts with news
of things to come?　　　Magnificat of ends;
she's yet to hear the word to contradict her death—

> *The curtain on the rise, her hands,*
> *both cord and cloth. And Friday slips, ajar.*

WHAT WE KNOW

The midday sun, the evening, and
the moon are pocket change and silver
in our hands; the late rose is the deep
rouge of a cheek, and autumn, speckled
squash in market carts; and when we
look above: Saturn spins the gold
rings on our hands.

Immediacy's a better kind of trust—
as when we reach the blue endangered
lake, its basin, the equator of new life.
How else to ponder here? What
might we think, when leaf and bird
are feather-bed and roost, no matter
what we name the remnant geese.

All this: the journey of a vast world
through our ears, whispered as breeze
and finishing as birth, while burrowed
deep in scapula and throat. *I know you
well, I know you in your skin, for where is
truth if not in wounds that heal, in wounds
that hide your racing, crimson yield.*

WHITE CROW

I

A bevy of crows in the moon-
light; nature hums her elaborate
pleasure in numbers.
      And in numbers
they flock, twitch
exactly to wishbone and plume,
equal luck.   Pluck a stone,

and a quiver of earthworms
uncoils into view, oiling
clay with their long, even
sundering.
      Strike a bone,
          and a starry-eyed mortal
will rise—godly wish

for a garden. (Ah, the secrets
a miracle breeds . . .)
      There's the bevy
again at departure,
and I count up the heads,
on a whim—
        wings that reach, leaves

          that weep:
moonlight darts, moonlight pins,
moonlight numbers.

II

I once learned, from a story,
that wildebeests saunter
away from their roots, horns
abloom, single-flowered.
      They trudge
into grasses for fruit—
now engaged, now adrift—

with their baby heirs balancing
losses—and they
          draw, and they drag:
all those wildebeests
pregnant in need, their sweet
births by the wayside.
      Think of this:

In the heart of their exile,
their numbers collapse—
        left to sully
their hooves in a trail's dust. . . .
      So, I look at the bevy
again; where the crows turn
their heads, not in envy, or fury,

or shame. Into daylight.

III

With the sunrise, the black
crows are gone; in their place,
a bright nestling, bright singular
shock:
      just a white bird.
(Tell me, what are the odds
of such whiteness surviving

apart?)
      And I think
(wouldn't you?) of endangered
young fathers and apricot brides,
speckled thumb-prints
and eggs . . .   ah, where nature
arrives, solely lovesick.

And she brings forth a child—
not a breed or a race, not
the pride or the spoil of invasion,
not a migrant whose burden
is tribe—
      just a child.
Oh, the beauty a bevy forgets,

pure, particular life.

CHILD'S FRUIT

Come, let me strain the raspberries
tonight, stir the sauce—glassy the sugar,
not too tart—pour it, wipe up the crimson
islands and return

to where I learned the revenue
of taste. Taste that's acquired an appetite
for place, rich with accrued mobilities:
sun on the slender sill at early day,

sun on the orange brick—mid-morn—
sun in the cordons of a slingshot noon
that settles on a dinner bell at dusk.
      A man's mind hovers

over brews and blends and recipes he
stored in sturdy, lifelong cabinets;
his lips keep company with old assorting
hands. How quickly he becomes, once

more, the hungry boy, perplexed by thick
and simple sweeteners. For him
someone has stirred, all day, all night—
long spoon along an earthen jar—this fruit.

A GHOST'S PROGENY

    We guessed the house would wince,
the wind would ride, and swift, around the corner,
a blue chant would mystify

the mortar: the ridges of our stubborn continent.
Once more, the world personified—I know;
I do this all the time—so come,

let's find ourselves in it. Perhaps the storm, eager
to batter homeward through the roof,
will miss your rubber boots, my shawls.

    I have a habit: to transpose
our hidden density on a sill, where a young woman
fills a stoneware dish with pie crust.

And, though she's twice-forgetful,
she'll have her mother's stance, a sturdy bearded man
behind her hips, kissing her shoulder.

She'll pull—so wifelike that we'll look away; he will,
of course, relish the skit and hour,
a summer under shingles, calling storms.

Yes, all at once their rainfall is *our* rain;
the house whose mortar winces rides our storm.
Forget the moon. Our room is full, is equally beholden.

> *As water reflects face back to face,*
> *So one human heart reflects another.*
> Proverbs 27:19

MADURODAM

—a city in miniature, near the Hague

In shadows lies the smallness
of our schemes: a tiny crest for tide,
a curlicue by hand,
streams of strolling lovers
with little overarching in their pose.

Our measure sings the whispers
of an architect uphill, a keeper
of details, the true and faithful finisher.
And yet, what might seem distant
to the daily meals we make—

split peas and shallots, cream or curd—
is proximate as summer herbs
until the summer ends.
        Out there, against a rail, a man
leans on his hunger and his bike,

just as, a hundred yards away,
a soup boils over in a farm—
which is why from afar,
he catches whiffs of family and birth,
and his careening stopped. *If only,*

oh, if only. . . .   The promise of a grander
scheme brings peril to Madurodam.
    Stir, pour, eat, love—
in this, our small-scale quivers,
and we glimpse, with eyes half-opened,

where a clink and consequence draw near,
where bits of railing prod.
    Life's here:
close to the leaning stranger
who understands our fear to hold, our *need*
    to hold his small but steady hands.

A VIABLE WAY HOME

A catapult to the border-shade: two cars ahead,
a slender gateway and then
a field. Is that our marigold backyard shield?
Honey, I'm home....

    A plump guard winks
    and thumbs the passport.

So cozy, the flesh—the old heart, driven;
the moment, brave. *Honey, I'm here,* called and
arriving to our wicker place:
the hunt for our cushions, our view of the wrens.

    Listen: the air is hinges-thin;
    it whistles a nest.

A lamp's incursion into the dusk alters the day....
Is that the moon?
One night, we turned the car around, as if we could,
I mean, really could persuade our manifold

    world to climb, eclipse our bones,
    fever the dust, eddying....

And that is—exactly—how we should rise;
the burial, a blitz; the skies, a grant of memory—

How else might we hurry home, unblind?

*You have seen many things but not observed them;
your ears are open but you do not hear.*
  Isaiah 42:20

ELENA FACES HALLOWEEN
(Or: The Quality of Here)

With the dawn comes a place, something
for her: a backyard, a house; hers, the province
she comes to. Yet, the rooms she remembers
are lifetimes away, even when the demand

of a child (trick or treat), just a frisk at the door,
is a peregrine wing on a street
leading home.   Rusted roofs, dusty
awnings: she left them believing the soil would

survive, some as head-dress or mask, or as skin
seeking cover in the cave of a hand, ever
closer.   Bird and story, recurrence of place
in the scope of the sky—autumn feast,

brooding flower—all under the moonlight
accruing and white, as it says: *where you hunger,*
there's seed; where you splurge and you spill,
where you dare drop a sweet, sight unseen,

there's your hour.   And the child,
without acre or grasp, only *luna*, burns bright.

THE WORLD YOU MAKE WITH LEAVES

> *Ah, but a man's reach should exceed his grasp,*
> *Or what's a heaven for?*
> —from "Andrea del Sarto," Robert Browning

One day you'll tidy up your home
and miss its trembling threshold—
though thresholds hold the delicate first
steps of lovers and of children.

One day you'll seek the welcome room
you owned, where little, errant feet
once crossed the floor but left no telling
echoes. And all because—

a threshold is the maple leaf
you pressed to make a parchment
lampshade; it is the panoply of leaves
from summers lost to autumn.

At times it gleams as an impatient
wish, an afternoon in heat, the forests
flamed, a tungsten close to burning. . . .
And other times, it embers.

So when your home is done—
breathless, the sway of doors, hinges ajar,
a proverb at each window—
perhaps you'll see the threshold wholly

still, still as the leaves
done dying on the sill, whose brink
is everything your fingers grasp:
                      all they will need, remember.

ANOTHER LIFE

—beyond the monastery walls

No white walls in the heaven of her thoughts; no oyster tiles, cold underneath her feet, no bare feet, come to think of it. No long contours or corridors to replicate her body's mute arroyos, small wrists with tender capillaries. . . .

The woman was a child of empty rooms; she held a chalk with forefinger and thumb and drew sweet, blushing faces.

No white winds in the heaven of her thoughts; instead, she's come into a rich and quaint hotel, pots filled with potting soil at every window. The lobby is crowded, like the cedar chests she left: two gowns, three christenings, one veil. . . .

The woman keeps her postcards in her purse, for memory is a travel she re-members, squinting at a far, outlasting glare.

Now heaven breaks the white walls of her thoughts, instead clear panels gather up her face: fine eyes and thick forgiving hair. If only she knew how or when, and in which pot, the earth will bear its best: its brilliant red geraniums.

AFTER-RAIN

The spell of after-rain:
deeper the bark, deeper the hair
when drenched, deeper the junipers

in their crawl, bristly and arduous.
After-rain: thicker the shades,
as molecules consume queryfuls of light,

with small, precocious answers.
How bruising-brave the larkspur's blue
becomes, how lover-heart

the roses—   And the fee?
Invasion, inhale, intake; a thirst to slake,
the fate all night avoids:
                the bonus of reflection.

ELENA'S REPRIEVE
(Or: The Quality of Return)

She's sitting where redemption set its bench,
beside a bed of news, a bin in verdigris
with piles that face retrieval.

Their pick-up is a last-chance bid, a merciful
release from what might fall
to those who wear and fray, who choose

a screened-in porch over the spare, wild weather.
Of course, she's pressed her fingers
on a tree and felt its fit; she's planted maples

every place they lived: three saplings
each, foot-stepping the yard with summer disks.
To save a breeze she trimmed

the lower limbs and watched the breeze become.
Often, the floating seeds gave lives
        she could not give.

But, oh, the confluence of *things*:
shawls and aprons blushing up the street, large
bags that dangle suppers, kitchens with ledges,

tiles, see-sawing shades; akimbo chairs and fans . . .
and, yes, those patios only humans build.
So, here she is, on this redemptive

bench, her name upon it.
You must return, it says; the roof is up,
the rooms are empty—and every homeward step
is home's reprieve.

> *God gives the lonely a home to live in. . . .*
> Psalm 68:6

EMMAUS

Spring is his burden and the night a robe: livid
as poppies in a roadside wrap, facing the dying weather.
Spring is the furrow on his shoulder swathe,
between the neck and forearm.

Thus was the intimation right: a savior comes
out of Jerusalem, with pericardial thread
to make a heart's claim: that history bears his thumb,
that saints soak up their suppers,

while the food, redolent on the table, aches for his hands.
And so he stops,
shuffling between a bramble and a gate, making as if
to leave, as if in earnest—

which means uncertainty rings true:
the crooked arm—*come near*—the branch that either
bleeds or flowers, the trickle fog.
    Ah, how the stars gallop off one another,

betting whether the men might, might not, will, will not
quiver the lock, set plates and cups and saucers.
The day is nearly over.
    The moon, struck briefly mute, takes heart—

EXCESS

for Jo

Spring in the garden edge, a periwinkle maze.
O Lord of spill and swell.   *I will not disappoint
you now*, he says; *I've honed your cell's repairs.*

Human ware is slippery in our hands; an ankle
twists, breaks on a granite ledge; joint
failure of a stone and heel, the puddled stairs. . . .

And so, God digs into his resurrection—
a funny rib and tooth, a good and solid shoulder:
the hidden measure of largesse.

Imagine, in a yard, another bone to spare; imagine—
long and grassy. For grasses err in favor
of excess. . . .   And isn't that the Word, *excess*?

  Not merely patched: pampered, festooned, unspent.
  A risen body, Lord, our flesh has never dreamt.

POSTPONEMENT

    I know you're here, enamored;
your land, a bevy of houses,
and by each gate, a rose bush,
and by each path, a lamp—
        always, on every table, the pitcher

        and a glass. I know a body's bliss
is thirst for moving closer,
to where a neighbor taps, taps on the window
sill. And that a visit tempts us
        to long stay-overs.

    This day, you'll be with me at last.

    Still, though I'm told a thief
broke, up the hill, impatient, I break
my fall again and splint the bones, aghast—
Yours is a world in wraps,
        the feast-in-foil: *Withholder*—

        my jug's juxtaposition
        to rivers through your hands.

LOVE AND THE AFTERLIFE

We'll spread last winter's needles on our soil
        and brave a new calligraphy of skin,

we'll take the early route with clipping
        shears, fill every vase with tulips.

A retinue of ants, hallway to aggregate,
        will turn into a lively pilgrim train—tip,

top, then puddle—laurel by the hedge,
        the tireless tortoise, its perennial brace.

April will snip the clouds
        to tiny rain—dew that is due,

lace looping nothing else, nothing that sheathes,
        hangs, after midnight scrims

before a clairvoyant, a star.
        Lawrence is piling mulch in gorgeous

heaps. What once was bark will animate
        a crib. Babies as plants,

and plants with baby feet.
    (Pale, before the bubbling witness.)

The garden hoists its seeds, its youngest peonies—
    our rake delays the clover

with its ribs.
    This much is heaven in our push and brink;

this much is world.
    For all the love we root in afterlife, time

to greet earthly flesh: here, we conceive
    a heart, here between fern and fence,

        the tenderest outlast—

A NOTE TO THE READER

The act of writing poetry is, for me, an emptying of self—a getting out of the way. In the poet's stead is the poem, which becomes a place of resonance, where the reader might recognize a voice otherwise unheard. For this to occur the poet must be *autobiographically silent*, so that the poems, individually and as a whole, transform into depositories for the reader's experience. The poem's truth is its emotion echoed in the reader, nothing else.

Resonance is relationship, and into this relationship, I pray, the Spirit comes. My hope is that *The Consequence of Moonlight* might be a poetic invitation to an awareness of this underlying Presence, as well as a call to be present as a loving witness to valuable and vulnerable things.

A realization of this resonance may be found in the name Elena, which plays a role in the shape of this collection. It is a name of old lineage, etymologically akin to the moon; probably from "ελενη" (*helene*), meaning "torch" or "corposant," and thus analogous to σεληνη (*selene*), "moon." The allusion to Elena, explicit in the opening section of the book, harks back to our being called by name. The first section of the book contains, among other poems and threading them, the poems of Elena. These are poems of self-discovery; they also give voice to a need to understand the self in a wider world.

The early clarity with which we hear our name often yields, of course, to doubt about our identity as we grow older; hence, Elena's absence in the second section of the book. But all is not lost in that in-between phase. This section contains various poems peopled by children. It is in the openness of childhood that our path toward rebirth might lie.

The poems in the final section start with a meditation before the Crucifix, for it is before the Sacrificial Corpus that we discover who we really are, through the One who calls us, tirelessly, by name. And so Elena re-emerges briefly in this section, when she is being called home, when she most needs to hear her name: at her moment of retrieval, her hour of grace.

The title of the collection, *The Consequence of Moonlight*, points to how the moon functions: she has no light of her own but lives on borrowed light, as we do. She is best perceived and most needed in the dark, fulfilling herself in absence. The moon is both luminous and obscure, generous and aloof, source of knowledge and evidence of mystery. She is all this, perhaps, because she must be *here* and *there*, orbiting the earth but not of the earth. And so, through her inherent paradox, the moon underscores a quality we rarely mention in our daily lives, but which the poems attempt to express as well: the quality of sainthood. Saints always meet the dark with light, yet their luminosity is often seen as lunacy in the world.

Finally, this is a collection about journeying, which points to the presence of Galicia, the northwestern part of Spain. Since the period of the Roman Empire, this was considered to be the end of the world; and as one of the most westward parts of Europe, the region known as Cape Finisterre—deriving from the Latin *finis terrae* or the "end of the earth"—has long been synonymous with outgoing and incoming journeys. From Galicia hundreds of thousands emigrated to the Americas and to the Philippines, particularly during the nineteenth century. Galicia also is the site of Santiago de Compostela, long held to be the burial place of St. James the Apostle, a destination for millions of pilgrims from around the globe, wherein they gather. Hence, its presence in the poem "Lessons from Galicia."

Sofia Starnes
Williamsburg, Virginia, 2018

ACKNOWLEDGMENTS

The author is grateful to those publications where several poems or variations of poems in this book first appeared:

A! Magazine for the Arts, "Why Honeymoons Are Brief"

America, "Emmaus," "Child's Fruit" (as "Visiting Day at Morningside")

ARTS, "Invitation," Pushcart Prize nominee, "The World We Make with Leaves"

Blackbird, "Last. Child. Last. Child."

caesura, "Child's Mourning Lesson"

Casa de Cinco Hermanas, "Elena by the Curb," "Elena Leaves Home"

Christianity & Literature, "Catacomb," "Another Life"

The Christian Century, "Excess"

The Cresset, "A Mode of Permanence"

Dappled Things, "Mushrooms," "Lessons from Galicia," "The Bridal Ferns"

Forum (Phi Kappa Phi), "A Child's Gethsemane" (as "Out of the Garden")

The Freeman, "The Genes We'd Choose," Pushcart Prize nominee

Ginosko, "Facing the Fire"

Measure, "The New World"

Mezzo Cammin, "Whole," "The Ways of Touch," "Where the Clover"

Moon Poems: An Anthology, "Elena Faces Halloween" (as "The Power of Here,") Pushcart Prize nominee

NLAPW Website, "Archetypes"

Notre Dame Review, "A Ghost's Origin"

The Pen Woman, "Tunnelers," "Elena's Birthday Part," "Survival at the Crossing"

Poems of Devotion: An Anthology of Recent Poets, "Close to the Tree"

Presence, "Unknowing"

The Sewanee Theological Review, "The Gatekeeper" (as "A Declaration of Intent")

Spiritus, "Baptism of Desire"

Studio Collective, "Tenebrae"

Sunstone, "Lunar Eclipse"

St. Bede News, "God's Renter"

Visions, "Love Poem"

War, Literature and the Arts, "O Vivifying Bones," "The Corporal's Wedding"

The William & Mary Review, "Emerge"

Windhover, "Chaos Theory"

Thanks are further owed to Franciscan University and to David Craig, poetry series editor, for publication of the limited-edition chapbook *Love and the Afterlife,* which featured a number of these poems, some in earlier versions.

ABOUT PARACLETE PRESS

Who We Are

As the publishing arm of the Community of Jesus, Paraclete Press presents a full expression of Christian belief and practice—from Catholic to Evangelical, from Protestant to Orthodox, reflecting the ecumenical charism of the Community and its dedication to sacred music, the fine arts, and the written word. We publish books, recordings, sheet music, and DVDs that nourish the vibrant life of the church and its people.

What We Are Doing

Books

PARACLETE PRESS BOOKS show the richness and depth of what it means to be Christian. While Benedictine spirituality is at the heart of who we are and all that we do, our books reflect the Christian experience across many cultures, time periods, and houses of worship.

We have many series, including *Paraclete Essentials*; *Paraclete Fiction*; *Paraclete Giants*; and the new *The Essentials of...*, devoted to Christian classics. Others include *Voices from the Monastery* (men and women monastics writing about living a spiritual life today), *Active Prayer*, the award-winning *Paraclete Poetry*, and new for young readers: *The Pope's Cat*. We also specialize in gift books for children on the occasions of Baptism and First Communion, as well as other important times in a child's life, and books that bring creativity and liveliness to any adult spiritual life.

The MOUNT TABOR BOOKS series focuses on the arts and literature as well as liturgical worship and spirituality; it was created in conjunction with the Mount Tabor Ecumenical Centre for Art and Spirituality in Barga, Italy.

Music

The PARACLETE RECORDINGS label represents the internationally acclaimed choir *Gloriæ Dei Cantores*, the *Gloriæ Dei Cantores Schola*, and the other instrumental artists of the *Arts Empowering Life Foundation*.

Paraclete Press is the exclusive North American distributor for the Gregorian chant recordings from St. Peter's Abbey in Solesmes, France. Paraclete also carries all of the Solesmes chant publications for Mass and the Divine Office, as well as their academic research publications.

In addition, PARACLETE PRESS SHEET MUSIC publishes the work of today's finest composers of sacred choral music, annually reviewing over 1,000 works and releasing between 40 and 60 works for both choir and organ.

Video

Our DVDs offer spiritual help, healing, and biblical guidance for a broad range of life issues including grief and loss, marriage, forgiveness, facing death, understanding suicide, bullying, addictions, Alzheimer's, and Christian formation.

Learn more about us at our website:
www.paracletepress.com or
phone us toll-free at 1.800.451.5006

SCAN TO READ MORE

ALSO AVAILABLE FROM PARACLETE PRESS

Communion of Saints
Susan Miller
978-1-61261-858-6 $18.00 Trade paper

"Old-world saints and soup-kitchen servers, a church in a dream whose congregants hold countless candles, and winter subway rides when lighting and faith flicker out. *Communion of Saints* represents an unlikely achievement: deeply spiritual and delicate poems that speak directly to our modern moment."
—Yehoshua November, author of *God's Optimism*

The Yearning Life
Regina Walton
978-1-61261-863-0 $18.00 Trade paper

"With a lover's attention to the beloved, Walton attends with both yearning and delight to the world at hand, apprehending the promise of that world's subtle but sure connection to the Love that moves all things."
—Scott Cairns, author of *Slow Pilgrim: The Collected Poems*

The Paraclete Poetry Anthology
Selected and New Poems
Mark S. Burrows, editor;
foreword by Jon M. Sweeney
978-1-61261-906-4 $20.00 Trade paper

Includes Phyllis Tickle, Scott Cairns, Paul Mariani, Anna Kamienska, Fr. John-Julian, SAID, Bonnie Thurston, Greg Miller, William Woolfitt, Rami Shapiro, Thomas Lynch, Paul Quenon, and Rainer Maria Rilke. "You'll wear out the pages and the binding before you're ever ready to put down this book."
—*Chicago Tribune*

Available through most booksellers or through Paraclete Press:
www.paracletepress.com   1-800-451-5006 | Try your local bookstore first.

www.ingramcontent.com/pod-product-compliance
Lightning Source LLC
Chambersburg PA
CBHW070847160426
43192CB00012B/2341